Prayers for Seniors

From Your Heart to God's Ears

Prayers for Seniors

From Your Heart to God's Ears

Linda Fagerland

Pleasant Word (a division of WinePress Publishing, PO Box 428, Enumclaw, WA 98022) functions only as book publisher. As such, the ultimate design, content, editorial accuracy, and views expressed or implied in this work are those of the author.

ISBN 1-4141-0605-X
Library of Congress Catalog Card Number: 2005909032

Table of Contents

Acknowledgments

I am so grateful for the help that I received in writing these prayers and putting this book together. I thank my daughter, Katie, for her help in data processing and my dear friend, Mary Glaeser, for her help in editing and formatting. I am thankful to my friend, Nancy Roberts, who encouraged me as I set out on this journey and for supporting me with her special talents in my times of need.

A special thank you to my husband, Jerry (Dear), for his heart for our seniors and the work that he does for them. His example inspired me to write these prayers.

Finally, I would like to give thanks to my Lord and Savior, Jesus Christ. He wrote these prayers; I simply put them down on paper.

Introduction

For many years of my life I thought praying was what you did when you wanted something from God. I hoped that maybe He would hear me and that He would answer my prayer, but in the back of my mind I figured, "He has more important things to tend to than my little wants and desires."

I began my walk with Jesus Christ at age forty, and then I began learning the truth about prayer. I studied what our Lord says about prayer in His Word (the Bible), and I became excited! Our Lord says that He hears the desires of the afflicted and He listens to our cries. Jesus Himself told us that anything we ask for in His name shall be done for us. I started praying for other people and for myself, and He was faithful and answered many of my prayers.

In 2002, my husband started a senior outreach ministry. As I began to spend time with the elderly, I was blessed to see the wisdom, compassion, and grateful hearts that were a big part of them. I also saw a lot of loneliness and despair, however. I often heard the question, "Why am I still here? Why doesn't God take me home?" During this time the Lord showed me the love He has for our elderly population, and He began to give me prayers to write specifically for them.

My hope for those who read these prayers is this: that as you pray, you will know with certainty that our dear Lord has His ear bent toward you as you talk to Him. He hears you, and He will be faithful to you by answering your prayers and by giving you the desires of your heart. He loves you and will never leave you or forsake you…that is His promise to you.

May God bless you and keep you all the days of your life!

Linda Fagerland

Chapter 1

Praise You!

I praise You for Your faithfulness.
I praise You for You are all powerful.
I praise You for Your glory and majesty.
I praise You for You are just.
I praise You for Your righteousness.
I praise You for You are the Prince of Peace.
I praise You for You are holy.
I praise You that You provide everything I need.
I praise You that You redeemed me from death.
I praise You for You possess all knowledge and wisdom.
I praise You for You heal…You are the Great Physician.
I praise You that You are everywhere. (You are here right now.)
I praise You for You are full of mercy and compassion.
I praise You that Your love for me goes on and on.
I praise You that Your Word is truth…You never lie.
I praise You, O Great Teacher!
I praise You that You are King of kings and Lord of lords!
Hallelujah! Amen!

Chapter 2

AS I BEGIN MY DAY

Lord, I thank You for all the new blessings that are waiting for me today. Help me to share those blessings with others whom I may come in contact with today. Help me to be kind and compassionate and not grumpy and mean. May those who see me today see the light of Jesus through me. Use me for Your purposes and for the advancement of Your kingdom here on earth throughout my day. I pray this in the name of Jesus. Amen.

Chapter 3

Putting on the Full Armor

Lord, I thank You that You equip me with all that I need to protect me from the enemy as I start this day.

I thank You for the belt of truth. May I walk with the Lord Jesus today who is the Way, the Truth, and the Life.

Place on my chest the breastplate of righteousness. I am secure in Your love as I wear this today.

Shod my feet with the slippers of peace. As I go out today, let me walk in the peace that surpasses all understanding.

Give me the shield of faith. As I hold this before me, any arrows that are shot at me from the enemy will be extinguished and fall to the ground.

Place on my head the helmet of salvation to protect the thoughts that go through my head. By wearing this, may I take every thought captive unto the King of kings, Jesus.

Finally, place in my hand the sword of the Spirit, which is Your Word, O Lord. Speak Your Word to me today as I need it, Lord, to fight against the presence of evil.

I thank You for this armor, Lord, as I begin my day.

All in the name of the Victor, Jesus Christ. Amen.

Chapter 4

As I Go to Bed

Dear Lord, I thank You for this day. I thank You for the good that I saw happen, and I also thank You for the bad; for I know all things work for the good of those who know You and love You. I thank You for using me today (even if I didn't notice it). May any words that You gave to others through me be planted firmly in their hearts.

Give me a restful night and hold me in Your arms as I sleep. In Jesus' name I pray. Amen.

Chapter 5

For Physical Healing

Lord, I come to You today to ask for Your hand of healing upon my body. I am having trouble with _______ (name your physical problem here). I have faith, Lord, that You can heal this, just as You healed so many in the Bible. Touch my _______ (part of body) and restore it to wholeness.

I will give You all the honor and all of the glory forever and ever. In Jesus' name. Amen.

Chapter 6

HEAL MY PAST, LORD

O Lord my God, You know what happened to me, that part of my past I have locked away that no one but me knows about. I have tried to hide it even from You, Father. I'm too embarrassed, too ashamed to even allow myself to bring it before You, my Creator.

But I am only kidding myself. Nothing is hidden from You, my Lord. You see when I come and when I go, when I sit and when I stand. Yes, You even see what I have kept hidden for so long.

I come before You now, Lord, because it is time. I want to be set free from what has held me in bondage for so long. Help me, Healer. Take the wounds of my past and shine Your light upon them. I do not want them any longer.

By Your Word I will be set free and totally healed. So I ask You now, Father...say the word and heal this child. I have faith and I trust in You, Lord Jesus. In Your holy and precious name. Amen.

Chapter 7

Prayer for My Marriage

Lord, I come to You today to pray for my marriage. Father bless _______ and me so that we may be the husband and wife that You intended us to be. I pray that there would be three of us in this marriage: _______, me, and Christ, and that Christ would be in the center of our union. I ask that when _______and I look at each other, that we would see You first. I pray that we would fall in love all over again, that You would ignite passion in us, Lord.

I thank You, Lord, for bringing us together. We met only by Your divine intervention. Bless us, strengthen us, and anoint our union so that we, as a couple, may bring You honor and glory for the rest of our days together. In Jesus' name. Amen.

Chapter 8

PRAYER FOR MY HUSBAND

Father, I do not even know how to begin to thank You for bringing my husband, _______, into my life. You truly do give me the desires of my heart, and _______ is one of those desires. He has been my comfort in times of sorrow, my strength in times of weakness, my advocate when others turned away, my support both financially and mentally, my lover, and my friend.

When I think back on our marriage, I can see not only the love that _______has for me but the love that You have for me, Lord. To give me such a gift is more than I deserve, but out of love You brought him to me.

Forgive me, Lord, for the times that I have not been the wife You intended me to be. I pray that You would show me how to be the most loving wife that I can be.

I pray Your hand of protection upon _______ today, Father. Shower him with the many blessings that You have for him. In Jesus' name. Amen.

Chapter 9

Prayer for My Wife

Lord, I just want to fall to my knees in thanksgiving when I think about how You brought _______ into my life. She truly is my "better half." I want You to know, my Lord, that I recognize how she has been there for me and has stood by my side during our life together—even when it wasn't easy to do. I ask, Father, that You would bless her in abundance for all those times she supported me.

I also realize, Lord, that I haven't always been the best husband that I should have been. I ask You to forgive me, Lord, and cleanse me of those times by the blood of Jesus Christ. Help me from this day forward to be a godly, gentle, and loving husband.

Protect _______ today from harm and wrap Your loving arms around her for I know that You love her even more than I do. I pray this for _______ in the name of Jesus. Amen.

Chapter 10

Prayer for My Son

Lord, I lift up my son, _______, to You today. I thank You, Lord, that You gave _______ to me. There have been good times and rough times in our relationship, but I recognize that he truly is a gift from You.

I thank You, Father, that You entrusted _______ to me as a baby. I pray that I raised him as You wanted. In my humanity, however, I made mistakes. I ask You to forgive me for the times I wasn't the parent that I should have been.

I pray Your hand of protection upon _______ today. Keep him safe from all sickness and harm. Lay Your hand of guidance upon him and set his feet upon Your path of righteousness. Bless _______, Lord. In the name of Jesus I pray. Amen.

Chapter 11

Prayer for My Daughter

Lord, I lift up my daughter, _______, to you today. I thank You, Lord, that You gave _______ to me. There have been good times and rough times in our relationship, but I recognize that she truly is a gift from You.

I thank You, Father, that You entrusted _______ to me as a baby. I pray that I raised her as You wanted. In my humanity, however, I made mistakes. I ask you to forgive me for the times I wasn't the parent that I should have been.

I pray Your hand of protection upon _______ today. Keep her safe from all sickness and harm. Lay Your hand of guidance upon her, and set her feet upon Your path of righteousness. Bless _______, Lord. In the name of Jesus I pray. Amen.

Chapter 12

Prayer for My Relative

Lord, I thank You for placing _______ in my family. I ask You, Father, to bless him/her today, to keep him/her safe, and to protect him/her from illness. I pray that You would touch _______ today and keep him/her far from the enemy's reach. Show _______ just how much You love him/her. I ask this in the name of Jesus. Amen.

Chapter 13

Frustration Over My Roommate

Lord, I come to You in frustration over the person with whom I have to share my home. If I step back to gain some perspective, I know that You assigned us together here. You, O Lord, are sovereign over all the earth...including my home.

I ask You, Father, to help me to see _______ with Your eyes. Help me to love _______ the way that You do. Guard my lips, Lord, that I would not say anything harsh to _______. Let my words be pleasing to You always.

By Your help and guidance, with my speech and my actions, may _______ come to know You as I do. Allow us to become not only true friends but family in the Body of Christ. Soften _______'s heart, Lord, so that he/she may receive Your words that come from my mouth. May those words be planted in rich soil. In the name of Jesus I pray this for _______. Amen.

Chapter 14

Thank You for My Roommate

Lord, I thank You for my roommate, _______. I know that You assigned us to live together. I pray, Father, that Your hand would be upon us both day and night. Lord, I desire that we would constantly pray together and sing praises to You together. Put Your words upon my lips when I speak to _______ and Your words upon _______'s lips when he/she speaks to me.

May Your presence fill our home every minute of every day so that we may live the rest of our lives in serving You. Bless _______, Lord. I pray this in the name of Jesus. Amen.

Chapter 15

Prayer for Protection

Lord, I come to You and ask for Your hand of protection upon me now. The enemy is trying to rob, kill, and destroy that peace that You offer me. I know that You are the Victor over darkness. Take me into Your refuge and shield me from all harm. Give me that peace that surpasses all understanding as I trust You and cling to Your robe. In Jesus' name. Amen.

Chapter 16

Prayer for My Salvation

Lord, I know that I am a sinner. I realize that I have grieved You by my selfishness in taking the easy way and succumbing to my earthly desires. Sin separates You and me, and I don't want to be separated from You anymore. I examine my sinful heart and confess my sins before You. (Take a moment to think about how you have sinned.) I now lay these sins at the foot of the cross.

Jesus, I understand that You left Your mighty throne in heaven, became a man, and died a horrible death on that cross so that I could be forgiven for these sins. Wash my sins away by the redeeming blood that You shed on the cross. Now I am clean! I am free!

Holy Spirit, come and help me to walk with You all the remaining days that I have here on earth. From this moment on I die to myself and my worldly desires, and I live for You and Your purposes for me. I thank You, Lord, that You are my Savior. Because You died and rose from the grave, I will be able to spend all eternity with You in heaven.

I pray all of this in the saving name of King Jesus! Amen.

Chapter 17

I'M SO GLAD YOU'RE IN MY LIFE, LORD

I thank You, Father, that You are in my life. I am so glad that You drew me to Yourself and brought me from darkness to light. I thank You that You have removed the scales from my eyes and that I can clearly see the wonders of Your love.

There is nothing more important to me than my relationship with You, Jesus. I thank You for dying on the cross so that I can spend all eternity with You. Until that day, Lord, may I proclaim to others all the rest of my days just what You have done for me. In Jesus' name. Amen.

Chapter 18

Speak to Me, Lord

You have said, Lord, that You will give us the desires of our hearts. I desire that You would speak to me, Your humble servant. Give me ears to hear, Lord, and I will listen. So this day, Lord, I will be attentive and wait and watch for that light for my path and that lamp unto my feet...Your Word. In Jesus' name. Amen.

Chapter 19

A Thank You Note to Jesus

I just want to thank You, my Lord Jesus. You are King of kings, and You sit on Your throne in heaven. But there was a time when You weren't on Your throne. You left Your reign as King to become a human being. You did this, Lord, with one thought in mind…me. You did this with one purpose at hand…the cross.

Jesus, You were born this beautiful little baby. Little did Your proud mother know that this night, the night of Your birth, was the beginning of Your journey to sacrifice Yourself in death for me. She didn't even know who I was…but You did.

You walked this earth, sweet Jesus, a perfect man. All You ever wanted was to glorify the Father while You were here. The Father, my Creator, the One who loved me so much that He wanted to send You, my Savior, my Redeemer. Thank You, Jesus, that until Your last breath You never once took Your sights off the reason You came…me.

You could have changed Your mind. You even prayed to the Father that He might give You another way instead of the brutal suffering and death that awaited You. But in the end, You pressed on up that hill, to the cross, to Your death for me. Thank You, Jesus, for not backing out. Thank You, Jesus, for saving my life.

Your child,

Chapter 20

A Prayer for Passing on Wisdom

As I sit here, Father, I sometimes feel pretty useless. Forgive me, Lord, because my pity for myself is an insult to You. The life You have given me so far has been full of blessings. I sit in awe of the wisdom that I have today compared to fifty years ago.

Lord, I come in contact with people every day of my life...the people who care for me, fellow residents, and the people who come to visit me. Am I passing on to them any of the wisdom or the blessings that You have showered upon me?

Father, I ask You to bring to my mind those important pieces of wisdom that You have put into my life over the years. Help me to know with whom and when to share these bits of wisdom and knowledge. I want to help others as You have so lovingly done with me. Thank You, Lord. In Jesus' name. Amen.

Chapter 21

Prayer for My Body

Lord, I look at this body now (sometimes in disbelief) and ask, "What happened?" I seem to have lost the ability to care for myself. Things as simple as tying my shoes and dressing myself have now become next-to-impossible feats for me.

Father, help me to remember that this is just my physical body. The body I have in heaven will be perfect. I will run back and forth along streets of gold. Help me to be strong in my mind and not pity myself, Lord. I thank You and praise You for the years of service You have given this body.

Lord, I pray now that You would minimize my physical pain. Through the Great Physician's name, Jesus, I pray. Amen.

Chapter 22

Sleep in Heavenly Peace

Lord, I have heard the song "Silent Night" hundreds of times. But I am focused now on the phrase "sleep in heavenly peace." Can there be anything as quiet, as calm, as comforting as heavenly peace?

Lord, tonight as I turn in, I ask for that same heavenly peace as I drift off to sleep. When I awake in the morning, I want to be totally refreshed and ready to begin a new day…a day that You have already created just for me. I pray this through Jesus. Amen.

Chapter 23

Give Me A Receiving Heart

Father, I come to You in despair and frustration. All my life You have allowed me to be a self-sufficient and independent person. I have been the caregiver for my family and for others. But now here I am, on the receiving end of needing care.

I confess that I am not doing a very good job of receiving that care. I am so angry that it has come to this. I need help doing all the things that I used to take for granted. But for some reason, Lord, You have allowed me to come to this place in my life.

I come to You to repent of my anger and my pride. In carrying this negative attitude toward those trying to care for me, I rob them of the blessings that You have for them through serving me. Change my heart, Lord, and help me to graciously receive whatever my caregivers have to offer. I want to be like Your disciples when You washed their feet.

You have brought me into a new season, and I want to honor You, Father, by living it well. I trust You and love You and implore this, Father, through Your Son Jesus Christ. Amen.

Chapter 24

Prayer for Salvation of a Loved One

Lord, I lift up _______ to You. Lord, _______ does not know who You are and refuses to listen to the truth about You. I pray, Father, that You would heal _______'s spiritual deafness and blindness. Let the scales fall from his/her eyes. Lay Your holy and blessed hand upon Your child, _______. Prepare and soften his/her heart.

Then, Father, place someone in _______'s path, someone whom You have chosen just for this purpose. With everything already in place by You, I pray that You would use this person to speak Your Word to _______.

I pray that by the grace of the Holy Spirit, the seed of Your Word would fall on fertile soil. May the watering of the Living God bring forth a blossom that is full of truth, joy, and love.

I pray that _______ would know without a doubt that he/she has been redeemed by the blood of the Lord Jesus Christ. I thank You that You do not want _______ to perish but to have everlasting life. I pray this to You, Father, through Your precious Son, Jesus Christ. Amen.

Chapter 25

I Need to Forgive

Father, I need Your help. I am holding in my heart today such unforgiveness for _______. I hold that unforgiveness captive, and I guard it to make sure no glimpse of forgiveness will ever creep in. I feel I am right in not forgiving _______ because he/she doesn't deserve my forgiveness. They haven't earned it, and the pain is so deep I could never release it.

But, Lord, I have this vision in my mind. It is You…and You are hanging on a cross. Blood is everywhere. Your face and Your body are disfigured from the beatings of the soldiers. Your head hangs down, but Your eyes look toward me. And You say to me, "I forgive you."

"But Jesus," I say, "I have done nothing to earn that forgiveness!"

Then, Lord, Your eyes drift over to _______, and You say to him/her, "I forgive you."

Father, if Your Son, Jesus, forgives _______, then I pray that You would give me the key to unlock the prison of my heart. I want to be able to look at _______ the way Jesus looks at him/her. I know, Lord, that by forgiving _______, I will set myself free from that prison of hate. Touch my heart this day, Father, and guide me through this process. Through Jesus' name I pray. Amen.

Chapter 26

An "I Forgive You" Prayer

Jesus, I know You died on the cross and shed Your blood for the forgiveness of sins. Father, _______ has sinned against me. So now, Lord, I take that hurt and pain that _______ caused me, and I lift it up for You to take.

Lord, I forgive _______. I will no longer carry the hate for him/her but will replace that feeling with the peace that You give me. I ask You, Lord, to bless _______. In the name of Jesus. Amen.

Chapter 27

Abba...Daddy

Oh, my Abba...my Daddy—take me in Your arms and hold me. Wipe away my tears and kiss my wounds and make them "all better." Rock me, Father, and sing to me lullabies of love until I go to sleep.

I feel so safe in Your arms. I feel so secure in Your embrace. Never let Your kisses and hugs cease. I pray this through Jesus Christ, my Lord. Amen.

Chapter 28

I Want to Be a Child Again

It says in Your Word, Father, that we must be like children to enter Your kingdom. I look back at the day that I first met You, Lord. And that is exactly how I felt…like a child. I looked at You as my Father, my Abba, my Daddy. I looked at You with awe, admiration, and complete trust.

Father, I want to be that way again. I want to trust You with all that I am. I want to know without a doubt that You have a wonderful plan for me. You have laid out a plan that You are in the process of carrying out, even now, as I pray.

I have no fear or doubts because You are my Father. I know that You will care for me no matter what. Renew my heart, Lord, and make me a child again. I ask this through Jesus Christ. Amen.

Chapter 29

I RECEIVE YOUR LOVE

Lord, to this very day, as hard as I have tried, I still cannot comprehend all the love You have for me. You left Your throne in heaven and became human only to die a horrible death…all for me. And not just for me, Lord, but for every single person on this planet.

As I pick and choose whom I will love and to whom I won't even speak, I look at You and am glad that You don't love that way. It's so hard for me to understand why You would love murderers, molesters, abusers, and sinners…let alone me! But Your Word tells me that You love me, so I believe that it is true.

So today, Lord, right here and right now, I close my eyes and open my hands to You and just receive the love that You pour out on me. (Take a few moments to receive His love.)

Thank You, Lord, for loving me with no strings attached. In Christ's name. Amen.

Chapter 30

What Can Separate Me from You, Lord?

Can death separate us, Lord? Can things in this life separate us? What about angels or demons? Can the present or the future separate us? Can powers of any kind separate us? How about the highest height or the lowest depth? Is there anything in all of creation that can separate us, Lord?

The answer to all of these questions is No...No...No. Thank You, Lord, that nothing is able to separate me from the love of God that is in Jesus Christ. Amen.

Chapter 31

My Sin Is Too Great!

Lord, my sin is too great. If people only knew what I have done, they would never forgive me. I am so ashamed that I hide my sin where no one can see it. I know You can see it, Lord, but if I don't think about it, then maybe You won't either.

I want to get rid of this guilt, Lord. This pain and this ugly feeling are too much for me to bear anymore! Help me, Lord. Help me to see that Jesus forgave the thief on the cross. That thief did something so horrible that he was sentenced to death for it!

You forgave Paul, Lord, who before his conversion persecuted and killed Christians! Jesus forgave the lady who committed adultery and was going to be stoned to death for it. In fact, You forgive everyone...if they only come to You, confess their sins, and ask for Your forgiveness.

I want to release this sin to You once and for all! The enemy keeps it buried and in the dark just to make sure I never let it go. Jesus, shine Your light on this terrible secret. I am human and have sinned horribly.

Your Word says that once You forgive our sins, You remember them no more. I take this sin and place it at the foot of the cross of Jesus where it belongs...once and for all! I let it go!

Now wash me, Lord. Wash me clean. Wash me white as snow. Clothe me in a pure white robe, stain-free and crisp and clean and pure. As You look at me now, Father, You see a sinless creature. You look at me and see Your Son Jesus because that is who You created me to look like when I was born. Sin has changed that appearance to You, Father, but now through the blood of Jesus, here I am again...standing before You as You smile upon me and tell me how much You love me.

I am *free!* I am released from my prison of sin by the blood of Jesus. He took the keys of salvation and released me! If I am freed by the Son, then I am free indeed! Thank You, Jesus! Amen.

Chapter 32

My Death Sentence

I sat in the courtroom, awaiting my sentence. The judge walked in and sat down. He looked at me and said, "For all the sins you have committed in your life, I sentence you to death."

I started to sweat profusely and got very sick to my stomach. I finally doubled over and began to sob like I had never sobbed before. The court guards came to get me to take me to the gas chamber.

"No! No!" I cried.

Suddenly a man named Jesus walked through the courtroom doors. He looked at me with very compassionate and loving eyes. I was unable to look away.

Jesus turned to the judge and said, "Your honor, I have come to take ________'s punishment. Tell the guards to release him/her and take me in his/her place."

"But, Jesus," the judge asked, "are You willing to go to the gas chamber and die?"

"I wouldn't have it any other way," Jesus answered.

Looking very puzzled, the judge asked, "Why?"

"Because I love _______ so much that I want him/her to live." The court guards took off my handcuffs and put them on Jesus. As they led Him away, He turned and looked back at me and said, "I love you."

Jesus, I love You too.

Chapter 33

Lord, Where Have You Gone?

My God, my God! Where are You? I am having trouble finding You. At this moment, Lord, I feel so lost. I remember those times when I just reached out my hand and You were there to take it. Now I reach out my hand, and I feel nothing but air. I need You, Lord.

I cling to Your Word, O Lord. "Seek and ye shall find" (Matt. 7:7). I am so glad that at times like this, when I'm feeling so lost, that You are faithful, Lord. You are my Shepherd. You will come to find me and bring me back to You. Until then, Lord, I will be still...and know that You are God. I ask for patience while I am wandering through the desert. In the name of my Shepherd, Jesus. Amen.

Chapter 34

WHEN I'M FEELING USELESS

Lord, I'm lying here and feeling frustrated because I cannot do a thing! I can't walk. I can barely communicate. How can I continue to serve You, my Lord? How can I do anything of value for anyone?

What's that You say, Lord? You want me to pray? Your Word does say to pray without ceasing. It also says there is power in prayer. I guess You do say that every prayer lifted up to You is heard and answered. Prayer must be very important when I look at the fact that even Jesus prayed.

OK, Lord. I hear You and I will pray. I will pray for my family. I will pray for my caregivers. I will pray for those who live here. I will pray for the people in my life whom I have been unable to forgive.

Father, You take action when prayers are lifted up to You. I don't have to have a great body to pray. My spirit is alive and vibrant and longs to serve You. So I will serve You the best way I can, Lord. I will begin today. I will pray. Direct my prayers in Jesus' name. Amen.

Chapter 35

When I'm Feeling Sorry for Myself

Lord, I am feeling so sad for myself today. I cry out, "Why can't things be like they used to be?" But You gently stop my thoughts of pity, Lord. You then turn my eyes toward the cross. I think about how Jesus knew what was coming and prayed to You, Father, that You would change it for Him.

Then I look as Jesus was whipped again and again until the flesh fell off His back. I look at His face as He walked down the road to Golgotha. I watch as He carried the beam to which His own body would be nailed. I listen to the very people for whom He would die, mocking Him and spitting on Him as He passed them on the street. Then I hear the mallet coming down on the nails as they pierced His hands and feet. And here I am...feeling bad for myself.

Forgive me, Father. When I look at what Jesus went through for me, I feel very ashamed for my complaining. But the good news is that I can right now, right here, stand under that cross and give my selfishness and pity to You, and You will nail it there...forever! Thank You, Lord, for what You went through...just for me! In my precious Redeemer's name...Jesus. Amen.

Chapter 36

When I'm Feeling Depressed

Lord, I feel so distraught and sad as if my life isn't even worth living anymore. My soul is so downcast. I don't even have the desire to pray. I barely have the energy to cry out to You, Father.

But You know my heart. You know my deepest thoughts. I cry out to You, Lord. Where are You? I need You. Even in the depths of my pain, somewhere in my soul, in my spirit, I know You are there.

You have said that You are with me always, and I know that You have never lied to me. I lean on Your words of comfort and healing now. When I fall, I know that You will pick me up. Your grace is sufficient. I know that I can rest in Your arms. I know that Jesus came so that diseases (yes, even depression) can be conquered.

Jesus, I put my depression in Your hands now. I ask You to intercede for me to the Father. Lift me up and restore my soul. Please, Lord, fill my darkness with Your light. Heal me, Lord. I ask this in the name of Jesus Christ. Amen.

Chapter 37

WHEN I'M FEELING UNCERTAIN ABOUT THINGS

Lord, today I am feeling uncertain about _______. Fill my heart with trust in You, Father. Help me to remember, Lord, that You are certain about everything! You hold all things great and small in the palms of Your hands. You are certainly not in heaven wringing Your hands about this situation.

Lord, my human weakness causes me to worry and causes my uncertainty. But I do know this, Father: I do not need to know the end of Your plan. I just need to remember that You are taking care of the plans that You have made, personally, for me. There is no place that I would rather be than in the palms of Your mighty, gentle, and loving hands. I place my love and trust in Jesus. Amen.

Chapter 38

For the Loss of a Loved One

My God, my God, I feel so forsaken. I cannot bear to live without ________. I still can't believe he/she isn't with me anymore. It just doesn't seem real to me. I expect ________ to walk in here any moment. And when I realize that he/she won't really walk in here, I cry all over again.

I miss him/her so much. I truly know what it is to have a broken heart. I want it to be the way it was, Lord. When I could talk to ________, walk with ________, and tell him/her I love him/her. Lord, I feel like this sadness is going to be a permanent part of my life now. If I could only have ________ back…just for a day.

But I know, Father, that this is part of life. To die is gain and to be in Your presence. I think of ________ with You now—in Your arms. The light of Your presence is warm and safe, and You have welcomed ________ home. He/she will have no pain or sadness. ________ will run on streets of gold and live in the place that You have prepared for him/her.

I come to You now, Lord, and ask for that same light in my heart. Bring me into Your holy arms of comfort. I thank You, Father, for placing _______ in my life. I know You brought us together. Maybe that is why it is so hard now that _______ is gone.

Thank You for the many blessings that were brought to me through _______. Thank You for the times we laughed and cried together, for the times we argued and made up, and for the times that we were each other's strength in times of sorrow.

Even though my rock on earth is gone, Lord, I have my Eternal Rock. I know that You will never leave me, and in my sorrow You will comfort me. Because I am still alive, I know that Your work through me is not complete yet.

Help me to grieve appropriately, Lord, and then help me to carry on Your work that is left for me to do here. May the focus soon turn from my sadness and sorrow to Your kingdom and Your glory. Thank You, Jesus, for being here. Amen.

Chapter 39

You Have Prepared A Place for Me

Here I am, Lord, in this tiny room. It's a far cry from the house where I used to live. Sometimes it makes me very sad. But then, Lord, I think of how temporary this room is. You have gone ahead of me and have prepared an absolutely beautiful room for me!

That room shines with Your glory and has no need for a moon or a sun. It is constantly aglow with Your presence. The streets are all so gold they have the look of glass. The walls are decorated with every kind of precious stone...sapphires, emeralds, rubies, and diamonds. And this, Lord, is the room in which I will spend eternity.

The room I live in now is for the moment. The room You have prepared for me is forever! The best part is that in that place I will see You and talk to You and eat with You and sing with You. Thank You, Lord, for taking care of all that preparation just for me. In the name of Jesus. Amen.

Chapter 40

As Death Nears

Dear Lord, sometimes I think that I am ready to come and see You, but at other times I am really afraid of dying. I have lived so many years in this body that I am afraid to let go of it.

Jesus, help me to see Your face and to keep my focus on You. That is my prize. That is what I long for. I long to run toward You as Your arms are stretched out to welcome me home. One day You will hold me in those same arms. I look up and see You smiling at me. I can't wait to see the place that You have specially prepared just for me!

Hold my hand, precious Lord. Do not let me go. I pray this to You, Father, as You lead me home. Through Your Son, Jesus Christ. Amen.

From the Author

My Dear Friends:

I want to ask you a question. If you died today, what would happen to you?

Maybe you don't know the answer, or maybe you just aren't sure. Well, I have good news for you. You can know for certain...today...right now! Our Lord Jesus gives us the answer. In the Bible, Jesus simply tells people, "Come."

He says it many times. He just wants you to come to Him. Come and talk to Him; come and sit with Him; come and worship and praise Him; come and lay your burdens down before Him. Just come. You don't have to get all dressed up or make yourself worthy first. Come, today, just as you are right now.

Did you know that Jesus created you? He knitted you together in your mother's womb. He created you in His image. He knows your heart, your very being, and soul. He gave you your eye color, your hair color, and your personality. He decided how tall you would be and the size of your feet. You are unique because you were created by the King of kings!

As a result of the fall of Adam and Eve, however, we are born with a sinful nature. Because our Creator is holy, He cannot be in the presence of sin. Our sin separates us from God. In spite of our condition, He still says, "Come."

Well, how do we do that? How can we go to heaven when we die? How can we reconnect with the One who created us?

We do that through the sacrifice of Jesus on the cross and through His resurrection to life after He died. He said, "I am the way the truth and the life; *no one* goes to the Father *except* through Me" (John 14:6).

My friend, if you are not sure about what will happen to you after you die, I invite you to come to Him now. Turn to and pray the *Prayer for My Salvation* written in this book. Then read the Book of John. If you do not have a Bible, ask one of your caregivers or someone whom you know, and they should be able to help you with finding one. Remember, He created you and wants a personal relationship with you. So don't wait; just come.

Your sister in Christ,

Linda